beach calling

A Devotional Journal for the Middle Years and Beyond

missy buchanan

UPPER ROOM BOOKS®
NASHVILLE

Cover design and hand-lettering: Jay and Kristi Smith, Juicebox Designs
Typesetting: PerfecType | Nashville, TN

ISBN (print): 978-0-8358-1877-3 | ISBN (mobi): 978-0-8358-1878-0 |
ISBN (epub): 978-0-8358-1879-7

Printed in the United States of America

Contents

Introduction

The voice of the sea beckons me to come, relax, and unwind from the spin cycle of everyday life. Something about the sand and surf speaks to my heart and refreshes my wilting spirit. But the beach also serves as a classroom where spiritual lessons for the journey of aging are offered. These lessons have surprised me, delighted me, confounded me, and inspired me. Most of all, they have reminded me that to experience these lessons, all I need to do is show up, sink into a beach chair, and open my eyes behind my sunglasses.

For almost two decades, my life and career have focused on issues of aging. As a middle-aged caregiver for my own aging parents, I went to the beach as place of respite. I was on a beach when I first felt a nudge to write about aging faithfully. Nine books later, I also speak at senior living communities, churches, and conferences across the world and regularly visit older adult friends in my community. Yet as a woman of the Boomer generation (born between 1946 and 1964), I understand why my peers resist the topic of aging and why they feel such angst at the thought of growing older. We shudder at images of physical loss and thoughts of decline and vow to do all we can to stay young. We refuse to contemplate dreadful thoughts of losing loved ones or enduring a life-changing medical crisis. But even amid our best efforts of eating right, exercising regularly, and using anti-aging products, aging comes anyway, like the unstoppable tide.

I wrote *Beach Calling* for you, and I wrote it for me. Perhaps you are lucky enough to be reading this book on a pristine beach. But even if you are reading it at a cluttered kitchen table with a cup of lukewarm coffee beside you, I hope the lyrical language of the sea will transport you to a beachside retreat and draw you gently into the deep water of each spiritual lesson. Some might call this book a side-door approach to a difficult subject, and it is. If you want to ponder what aging faithfully means, you will want to read this book. If you find accepting or acknowledging your own aging journey to be difficult, you desperately need to read this book.

Don't rush through this devotional journal. Take your time, allowing the lessons to seep into your soul. As with poetry, the messages in this book have been distilled into few words that point to larger truths about life, loss, aging, and faith. Each meditation includes italicized scripture verses that I have woven into the text, creating an ebb and flow between my words and thoughts and God's Word. I hope you will feel prompted to open your Bible and study each passage in its full context. Each devotion ends with a series of questions to inspire you to capture your innermost thoughts in the journaling space.

It's time to kick off your flip-flops. Feel the sand between your toes. Let's walk together toward the open sea. The beach is calling.

Holy Paradox

In the first blush of light, I pause at the water's edge, letting the
cool foam lap my bare feet. My only companions at this
early hour are a few squabbling sanderlings, racing the tide.
Slowly I scan the horizon and look up to the heavens to try to
take in the vastness of the sky.
Standing before the magnitude and mystery of creation, I close
my eyes and let the sun's faint rays fall across my face.

By the word of the LORD the heavens were made,
and all their host by the breath of his mouth.

I open my eyes and gaze across the water that stretches as far as I
can see, reflecting the brightening sky.

Where were you when I laid the earth's foundation?
Tell me, if you understand.

It seems a holy paradox.

Standing at the water's edge, I am so small and insignificant in the enormity of creation; yet somehow it feels as though this majestic scene was made just for me.

Gentle waves crawl onto the sand like outstretched fingers, yearning for another's touch.

I dig my feet into the sand and grab sand between my toes, then release it like a toy crane letting go of its prize in an arcade game.

A deep peace washes over me. Grab and release. Grab and release.

As each grain of sand falls from my curled toes, I feel the pressure of to-do lists and schedules fall away.

Social media posts, medical appointments, family responsibilities—they all fall away beneath this watercolor sky.

The beach is my special meeting place with God.

It is my place of renewal and rest.

It is where I come to seek wisdom for the journey of life.

Returning to my low beach chair, I am keenly aware that getting up again will challenge my creaky knees.

But in this moment, I choose to bask in the holiness of the live performance staged before me.

Be still, and know that I am God!

For as the heavens are higher than the earth,

so are my ways higher than your ways

and my thoughts than your thoughts.

*Psalm 33:6; Job 38:4 (NIV); Psalm 46:10; Isaiah 55:9

— ◆ —

Let's tune out the distractions of the world so we can focus on God's creation spread before us. When we seek God's presence wherever we are, we receive calm assurance that God's ways are higher than ours. May we inhale the holiness of each moment and exhale our weariness and worry. Let us be still and know who God is.

— ◆ —

Why do you feel drawn to the beach?

How is God's presence different at the beach than in other places?

At this stage of life, how do you experience the beach differently from when you were younger?

Describe a time when you recognized the holy paradox of feeling insignificant and highly valued at the same time.

How does the beach prompt you to confront your own mortality?

Low Tide

Twice a day, the tide is pulled out to sea, leaving a wide stretch of
   sand for beachcombers to explore.

In the wake of the receding waves, I bend down to examine the
   shallow pools of saltwater and remnants of sea life left
   behind.

Things once hidden below the waves are visible now, exposed and
   vulnerable, until the tide rushes in again.

*Nothing in all creation is hidden from God's sight. Everything is
   uncovered and laid bare before the eyes of him to whom we
   must give account.*

My mind is drawn to occasions in the past when I felt vulnerable
   and defenseless—times of poor decision, rejection, and
   disappointment throughout the years.

This melancholy moment of reflection redirects my thoughts to
something deep inside.

Staring into the tide pool, I open myself to the truth of the
fragility of life.

Man is like a breath;
his days are like a passing shadow.

Life is brief, and aging is real. I feel it in my joints. I feel it every
time I lose my reading glasses or when I hear that another
friend has died.

Yet somehow just acknowledging the reality of aging is liberating;
I don't want to pretend to be young.

I want to be bold enough to be authentic; I want to be faithful
enough to prepare for life's challenges.

Some say that growing old is too depressing to ponder.

But here at the beach, I confront an important truth: To be
strong, I must first be vulnerable.

Like the creatures in the tide pools, I am designed to adapt to my
circumstances.

Soon enough the rising tide will return, bringing cool water to
refresh and renew my spirit.

So we do not lose heart. Even though our outer nature is wasting
away, our inner nature is being renewed day by day.

Bathed in the mystery and beauty of this place, I feel fully alive
and give thanks to the One who turns the tide.

*Hebrews 4:13 (NIV); Psalm 144:4 (ESV); 2 Corinthians 4:16

—o—

We will face trials in the future just as we have faced them in the past. Growing older will not always be easy. There will be times we feel vulnerable, but we can be certain that God is with us and that the tide will always return to refresh our spirit. Instead of focusing on the losses that may come with aging, let's hold onto God's promise of renewal and faithfulness.

—o—

Write about a time when you felt exposed and vulnerable. What did you learn?

How does growing older make you feel vulnerable?

In what ways are you being realistic about the challenges of aging? In what ways are you denying the realities of aging?

What changes are you likely to experience as you age?

How can you adapt to each transition that comes your way?

Simplicity

Beach life is an exercise in simplicity, encouraging me to strip
away the complications of an over-scheduled, digital
existence.

Here at the seashore, life is about flip-flops, sunscreen, a straw
hat, and a gauzy cover-up over a damp swimsuit.

It's about books, earmarked and stained with saltwater, and
guilt-free time to sit alone with my thoughts.

Why does it take the call of the surf to bring me back to what I
already know?

The good life is the simple life.

So I kick off my well-worn flip-flops and trudge barefoot through
the soft, deep sand to a place where the path opens to the
wide beach.

Suddenly I am aware of a breeze lightly brushing my face, causing me to stop midstride.

My eyes take in the trinity of sky, sea, and land.

The three converge in this holy place, an idyllic scene filled with the cries of seabirds and the promise of a beautiful day.

Sinking into a comfy chair, I close my makeup-free eyes.

The beach is a place where doing nothing points me to the most important things of life: relationships, family, and friends; compassion, forgiveness, and love.

For where your treasure is, there your heart will be also.

Here in this sandy corner of the cosmos, the Creator once again puts life into perspective for me.

Simplicity is about focusing on things that have eternal value.

For we brought nothing into the world, and we can take nothing out of it.

Basking in the mellow morning sunlight, I rediscover a deep thirst for greater simplicity as I grow older.

My thoughts wander ahead to a sobering truth:

One day, the stuff of my life will be hauled to the curb. Or boxed up and donated or sold.

Listening to the concert of the sea, I realize just how little I need in order to live a life that overflows with meaning and purpose.

*Matthew 6:21; 1 Timothy 6:7 (NIV)

—◯—

Seeking a life of simplicity may seem easy at the beach, but it is considerably more difficult in everyday life at home. The simple life is not just about decluttering our home each spring or donating old clothes we no longer wear. To live a life of simplicity is to be intentional about making more room for what really matters and releasing what does not.

—◯—

Write about a time of relaxation when you allowed your mind to wander and it led to a life-changing realization.

How do you currently deal with the clutter in your life?

Consider the possibility that your family members will not want or need your possessions after you are gone. How does that make you feel? Why?

What can you do to practice simplicity and cultivate an attitude of contentment as you grow older?

Which possessions could easily become burdens as you age?

Beach Time

Stretched out on a bright blue lounge chair, I close my eyes and let
my mind drift like the passing clouds above me.

I am delightfully unaware of the passage of time as the ocean lulls
me into that glorious state of calm and relaxation.

No clock. No watch. No alarm to interrupt my thoughts.

Time at the beach meanders like the pleasant fog of a daydream,
where hours and minutes carry mystery instead of linear
meaning.

A thousand years in your sight
are like a day that has just gone by.

Before pulling the sunglasses from the top of my head, I open my
eyes and let them adjust to the sunlight.

The peaceful view brings clarity to my muddled, finite mind.

The path to wisdom is not ticked off in hours or minutes.

Here at the seashore, the sights and sounds blend together to
create a sun-drenched retreat for deep thoughts to be born.

In fact, the only way to squander time at the beach is to believe
that I must do something to prove my productivity.

In this holy state of idleness, I am attuned to hear God's voice.

*Call to me and I will answer you and tell you great and
unsearchable things you do not know.*

Day by day, I am learning that having a keen awareness of my
own mortality keeps me from frittering time away on
insignificant things.

*Teach us to number our days,
that we may gain a heart of wisdom.*

I grab a handful of sand and funnel it through my fingers as if it
is falling through an hourglass.

Silently I give thanks that *kairos*—God's time—is not bookended
with birth and death.

From everlasting to everlasting.

And I remember that the most valuable commodity I have to
share with others is my time and attention.

*Psalm 90:4 (NIV); Jeremiah 33:3 (NIV); Psalm 90:12 (NIV); Psalm 90:2 (NIV)

— ◆ —

Though our chronological perspective of time—that is, *chronos*—is
limiting, it measures the world in which we live our days. When
we embrace the reality that life is finite, we can begin to live more

fully. Slowing down allows us time to think more clearly and to invest in meaningful relationships and new discoveries.

— ○ —

What tensions do you experience in daily life that relate to time?

Make a list of ten things you need to say no to if you want to spend your time on what is most meaningful.

Describe how an awareness of your own mortality can keep you focused on what is most significant in life.

Write a letter to your thirty-year-old self about what matters most to you.

Describe what your life might be like one year from now if you allow the lesson of the beach to help you reprioritize your time commitments.

Grace upon Grace

Standing at the water's edge, I squint into the bright sun and
  study the ocean as far as I can see.

The sky and sea blur together at the horizon, both vast blankets
  of never-ending blue.

As my eyes move closer to the shoreline, the water changes to
  turquoise with waves that tumble, pale and frothy, onto the
  sand.

Watching the surf is both mesmerizing and oddly reassuring—the
  uneven rush of water, waves that overlap one another,
  swells interrupted by the wake of a passing boat.

One wave flows in; another recedes.

Wave upon wave, the ocean rolls onto the sand.

From his fullness we have all received, grace upon grace.

The waves are like God's glorious grace, rushing in again and
again.

From the boundless heart of Creator, grace flows in, filling my
emptiness.

Waves of grace come when life is beautiful and bright. Waves of
grace come when life is cruel and unfair.

Letting out a long breath, I wade into the ocean until I feel the
cool water around my waistline.

I struggle to keep my balance in the continuous push of the waves
and stumble upon fresh insight about aging.

Perhaps God is teaching me to be less dependent on my own
power so that I will recognize my dependence on God's
abundant grace.

I have made you and I will carry you;
I will sustain you and I will rescue you.

As I look out to the open sea, my mind collides with the profound
mystery of the depth and breadth of the ocean—and the
depth and breadth of God's grace.

I lift my feet and sink into a curling wave, letting it pull me down
until I am completely covered by the cool water.

God's grace has carried me through the dark days of my past;
God's grace will carry me through the unknowns of the
future.

For it is by grace you have been saved, through faith—and this is
not from yourselves, it is the gift of God.

I rise from the sea with water dripping from my smiling face.

As I stagger through the waves back toward the beach, I feel the
pulsing tide push me along.

The flow cannot be stopped; it is a gift of grace.

*John 1:16 (ESV); Isaiah 46:4 (NIV); Ephesians 2:8 (NIV)

Grace can be a nebulous concept. How baffling to think that
we cannot earn God's endless flow of love, compassion, and
forgiveness. Textbook explanations of grace cannot adequately
describe the times we have experienced grace, especially in those
moments when we knew we least deserved it. Nevertheless, when
we cried out to God for grace, grace came rushing in.

Describe a time in your life when God's grace was unmistakable
and carried you through a difficult season.

Write about a time when your own sense of self-reliance caused
you great pain. What lesson did you learn from that
experience?

How would you explain the mystery of God's grace to a child?

List five ways you can be more intentional about leaning on God's
grace as you age.

Describe how your life would be different if you let go of your
desire for self-sufficiency.

Table

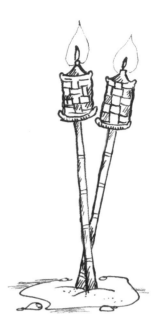

The scene from my front porch is one worthy of a magazine cover:
a long wooden table at the water's edge, beautifully set for
twenty guests, covered in white linens, dinnerware, and
rows of sparkling glasses.

From my perch, I can feel my heart swell as I watch a middle-
aged woman in a flowing white dress light the torches that
surround the enchanting sight.

I can't help but wonder if the dinner marks a milestone birthday
or anniversary.

Or perhaps this magical setting offers an extraordinary way
for friends and family to come together on an ordinary
evening.

Even before the last torch flickers with light, guests of all ages
start arriving, dressed in hues of khaki and white, leaving
their sandals behind to walk in the sand.

If we walk in the light, as he is in the light, we have fellowship
with one another.

Watching the joyful arrival, I feel a twinge of envy and a strong
yearning to gather with my own family and friends.

Why wait for the holiday frenzy to carve out time to be together?

Though some of us are separated by hundreds of miles, I yearn
for us to gather around the table on ordinary days, just to
celebrate love and life.

Even as the sunset fades to night, I can clearly see the love in the
faces of those around the table, reflected in the warm glow
of the torches: children, young adults, middle-agers, and
elders.

A new command I give you: Love one another. As I have loved
you, so you must love one another. By this everyone will
know that you are my disciples, if you love one another.

Their conversations are muffled, but I can imagine funny stories
and poignant remembrances being shared, binding them
together, heart to heart.

My eyes are drawn to an older woman seated in the center of
the table, perhaps the matriarch of the family or a great-
grandmother.

I watch her turn her head to gaze upon all the faces around her
before smiling contentedly to herself.

In this thin place where heaven seems so close, I let myself peer
wistfully into my own future.

If one day I become stooped and gray, I hope for opportunities to
gather at a table where love abounds.

There, I know my aging spirit will be nourished.

*1 John 1:7 (NIV); John 13:34-35 (NIV)

— ○ —

The table is a place of connection and blessing, especially when
family and friends of all ages are gathered around it. An overflowing
table is a symbol of God's abundant grace. In today's busy world
with family members and friends living far from one another,
creating regular opportunities for fellowship can be challenging.
Even so, participating in community is vitally important to the
journey of aging.

— ○ —

Why or how does this beachside reunion appeal to you?

Write about an especially memorable meal you shared with
family and friends in the past. How did this experience
create a "thin place"—that is, a place where heaven and
earth meet and where God feels close?

Make a list of people with whom you would like to share a meal,
God's love, or community.

If you found yourself as the oldest person at a table filled with
family and friends, how would you feel?

Describe any dysfunction or pain in your family that needs to
be addressed before you can feel a sense of well-being for
the journey of aging. What could be the first step toward
reconciliation?

Afternoon Storm

I wake from a catnap on the beach to see that the ocean has
    become moody in the thick, humid air.
It had been a beastly hot afternoon under a magnificent blue sky,
    but now I hear the deep rumble of thunder as dark clouds
    accumulate in the distance.
The sea is agitated, like rush-hour traffic at the beginning of a
    holiday weekend.
The wind picks up and, within moments, it is heaving and
    untamed, uprooting a row of beach umbrellas haphazardly
    planted in the sand.
Along the shore, people hurry to gather colorful towels and beach
    chairs before dashing for cover.
With the storm coming so quickly, I suppose I should leave too.

But something within causes me to linger for a few moments, watching the activity swirl around me.

An hour or so ago, I was lulled to sleep by the comforting rhythm of the waves.

Now the steel-gray surf is slapping the sand, sending spray across my face as the wind whips my hair.

I am reminded of how quickly life can change.

Life can go from brilliant to brutal in the blink of an eye: a devastating diagnosis, the death of a loved one, a dreadful accident.

A windstorm swept down on the lake, and the boat was filling with water, and they were in danger. They went to him and woke him up, shouting, "Master, Master, we are perishing!" And he woke up and rebuked the wind and the raging waves; they ceased, and there was a calm. He said to them, "Where is your faith?"

As I pull a beach towel over my head to shelter myself from the rain that has begun to fall, I glance up to see a line of birds on the rooftop of a nearby cottage, facing the wind.

I remember what someone once told me: Birds often face the wind during a storm to reduce their resistance to it.

Once safely inside my cottage, I begin to wonder. Am I faithful enough to face my own mortality?

Am I courageous enough to stare squarely into the uncertainty of my later years—the physical challenges, the loss of loved ones, the diminished independence?

Stand firm in the faith; be courageous; be strong.

After the storm passes, I step outside to take in the splendor of a

rainbow and the heavenly scent that follows the rain.

The chirping birds soar above the ocean, and a grin begins to

stretch across my face.

*Luke 8:23-25; 1 Corinthians 16:13 (NIV)

— ○ —

It takes courage to be realistic about the changes that come with aging. We would rather not think about unpleasant eventualities to come, so we usually try to avoid thinking about aging at all. Even so, we are acutely aware of how our bodies have changed over time. May we remember that God designed aging. We can find purpose in this journey if we open ourselves to new possibilities.

— ○ —

Write about a time when your life changed unexpectedly in just a

matter of minutes.

In what specific ways can you prepare yourself mentally,

emotionally, and spiritually for the challenges that may

arise on the journey of aging?

Make a list of ten things you fear most about growing older.

Make a list of ten things that you look forward to about growing

older.

Think of people you know who are courageously and boldly

facing the challenges of later life. What lessons can you

glean from their experiences?

Wonder

From the corner of my eye, I see a trio of children playing on the
beach within sight of their watchful parents.

For the past half hour, the youngest has been chatting nonstop,
providing commentary as she digs trenches in the sand
with her hands and watches them fill with water.

The middle child has his feet firmly planted in the surf and is
tracking a palm frond riding the tide.

The oldest child is sitting on the sand, focused intently on
creating a mandala-like circle of seashells and rocks.

All three are lost in the pure joy of the moment, oblivious to
unidentified beachgoers like me who watch them in awe.

There are no plastic toys in sight. No digital games or electronic
devices, at least for now.

The children are totally immersed in the natural wonders of the
beach, and, likewise, I find myself caught up in their wonder.
Studying the children at play stirs up a question: Why do adults
tend to lose that sense of childlike wonder over the years?

Look to the LORD and his strength;

seek his face always.

Remember the wonders he has done.

When did I decide that bending over and searching the sand for a
piece of frosted sea glass was too much trouble?
Why am I not exploring the sand with my feet, as if investigating
the surface of the moon?

Have you comprehended the vast expanses of the earth?

Tell me, if you know all this.

Today I intend to reclaim the wonder of childhood. I will get
up from my beach chair and step out of my comfort zone,
asking God to restore my sense of wonder.
I will hold seashells in my hands and study the intricacy of each
one.
I will throw out misconceptions that tell me that maturing years
are dreary and monotonous.
Wonder is that divine spark that awakens my curiosity and
deepens my awareness of God.
As I get to my feet and brush the sand from my legs, I think back
to Socrates.
Perhaps wonder really is the beginning of wisdom.

*Psalm 105:4-5 (NIV); Job 38:18 (NIV)

—o—

How easily we find ourselves in a rut. We seek the comfort of what we know and understand. But too much familiarity can leave us feeling lifeless, bored, or even jaded. The beach is an ideal place to activate our sense of wonder and open ourselves to new ideas.

—o—

What can you do differently today to intentionally bolster your sense of wonder?

Write about something you enjoyed as a child that you haven't done in years. What keeps you from doing it now?

Describe a time when you found yourself in a spiritual rut.

Write about what God is teaching you about wonder and awe during this season of life.

Describe how the trajectory of your life will change if you maintain a sense of wonder as you age.

Sunrise, Sunset

In the dark before the dawn, I step outside in my seersucker
pajamas, using the light of my smartphone to guide me.

The air is thick with humidity as I shuffle across the deck, feeling
the grit of sand on my bare feet.

At this early hour, the white curls on the tumbling surf are barely
visible, but I can hear the steady rush of the waves.

I settle into the solitude and keep an eye on the eastern sky as I
wait for the coffee maker to beep.

Within a quarter-hour, a golden glow begins to illuminate the
horizon, chasing away the murky darkness until the sun
finally makes its appearance.

I snap a few photos, then sit back to sip from my souvenir mug,
savoring the changing scene as light spills across the waves
and sand.

I am struck by how quickly the sun is rising now, setting the new
day aglow with light and hope.

The stunning panorama tugs at a memory from another time,
another beach.

I pick up my smartphone and quickly scroll through my photos
until I find an image of a magnificent sunset.

Just as I remembered, the blazing sun hangs low over the sea at
the day's end, as if it is melting into the water.

I hold up my phone, comparing the sunset photo to the real-time
sunrise before me.

From the rising of the sun to the place where it sets,
the name of the LORD is to be praised.

Sunrise and sunset mark opposite ends of each day, yet each
equally inspires me.

I was young and now I am old.

Daybreak and dusk. Young and old.

By God's design, each one mirrors its opposite in beauty.

In the gentle light of dawn, I embrace God's truth. Indeed, the
sunset is just as magnificent as the sunrise.

Do not fear, for I am with you;
do not be dismayed, for I am your God.

I do not have to fear the journey of aging. God will never leave me.

Instead of being fearful, I can seek the beauty that comes at the
end of each day just as I do at the beginning.

I can find beauty in both beginnings and endings.

*Psalm 113:3 (NIV); Psalm 37:25 (NIV); Isaiah 41:10 (NIV)

—o—

In our younger years, we experienced anxiety as the lazy days of summer drew to a close and the unknowns of a new school year loomed ahead. We suffered from the Sunday night blues, dreading the following day and a new workweek. As humans, we often think that the end of something good is reason to fret or be anxious. God reveals to us through the equally stunning images of a sunrise and sunset that in every ending there is a new beginning full of hope and promise. God's constancy will never fail us.

—o—

For a series of days, get up early to watch the sunrise. Make notes about the changes in light and the colors you observe. Take a few photos. Then, repeat your actions for the sunset. Write about each experience, comparing and contrasting the sunrises and sunsets.

How do you experience beauty, hope, and gratitude in the sunrise and the sunset?

How can the end of life (the "sunset") have as much purpose and beauty as the beginning of life (the "sunrise")?

What makes growing older a beautiful, purposeful, and worthwhile experience for you?

Write a letter to your future self with reminders that God designed the later years to be as inspiring as the early years.

Relentless

Today is one of those picture-perfect days at the beach, the
kind the visitors' bureau likes to promote in its colorful
brochures.

No crowds. No seaweed or riptides. No loud music or people
hawking trinkets.

Just pristine sand surrounded by palm trees waving in the soft
breeze and crystalline blue water.

I survey the magnificent ocean stretched out before me.

The swells rise and form waves that spill onto the sand.

The water is so clear that I wonder if my eyes are deceiving me.

From my beach chair, I hear the waves kiss the shore again and
again, providing a soothing soundtrack to my drifting
thoughts.

I am the Lord your God,

who stirs up the sea so that its waves roar.

The waves persist even when I am not paying attention. They
are relentless in their pursuit of the shore. Sometimes they
arrive in powerful surges, other times in long rolls or gentle
pushes.

They come ashore unceasingly. Persistently. Faithfully.

The tide is much like growing older.

Aging comes whether I notice it or not. It doesn't stop to ask for
permission. It cannot be turned off like a faucet.

Like the waves, it comes continuously and steadily, just as God
designed it.

Why, then, do I try to stop aging as though it's a disease from
which I need a cure?

The rhythm of aging is like the ebb and flow of the sea.

In aging, as in life, I've experienced undeniable loss and
unimaginable blessing; I have felt sorrow and immense joy.

Even to your old age and gray hairs . . .

I am he who will sustain you.

The beach calls me to a life of promise.

Just as the tide of aging persists, so does the faithfulness of my
steadfast God.

*Isaiah 51:15 (NIV); Isaiah 46:4 (NIV)

—◇—

We often try to avoid our fears about aging. We believe that we can control the coming days, months, and years—as if we can control the ever-moving tide. Trying to stop the waves is useless. We cannot battle aging as if it is an enemy, nor can we control what is to come. God designed our bodies to change over time, and every season of life holds sacred purpose.

—◇—

When you see an older adult using a walker or a wheelchair, how do you feel? Why?

How is God's perception of aging different than culture's view of aging?

How has culture negatively influenced your perception of aging?

What do you think God wants you to learn from the journey of aging?

When and how have you witnessed God's persistent faithfulness in your life?

Silence

I come to the beach seeking peace and quiet in a chaotic world
where politicians and newscasters bicker 24/7.

The noise of the world wears down my spirit like waves that crash
onto a rocky cliff that juts out into the sea.

Yet when I shut my eyes to the early morning sun and listen, I
realize that the beach is never quiet—not really. The sounds
of nature do not cease.

I decide to make a mental list of each sound I hear.

The whoosh of waves, repeating like an ancient chant. The
squawk of a solitary seagull in the distance. The gentle
flutter of palm trees in the breeze. The splash of a
beachcomber's feet in the shallow tide pools.

The voices of the beach sing to me, and I whisper a word of
thanks.

Be filled with the Spirit, as you sing psalms and hymns and
    spiritual songs among yourselves, singing and making
    melody to the Lord in your hearts, giving thanks to God
    the Father at all times and for everything in the name of our
    Lord Jesus Christ.

I think of a friend who plays recorded sounds of the ocean at
    night to fall asleep—to cover the noise of the world.

White noise, she calls it.

Perhaps silence is not really the absence of sound but the absence
    of noise.

I open my eyes, noticing how the water is a richer blue in the
    growing light.

Up and down the shore, other early risers are dragging their
    beach chairs through the sand, but the breaking waves
    drown out the sound.

In my daily life, I am tempted to fill any quiet moment with noise,
    trying to distract myself from the reality of an empty house
    now that my children are grown and have moved away.

But surrounded by the music of the beach, I am mindful that
    silence is vital to my spirit.

He restores my soul.

He leads me in right paths
    for his name's sake.

Here at the beach, I savor the waves' restorative sounds—not the
    noise of the world but the gentle whisper of creation.

*Ephesians 5:18-20; Psalm 23:3

—o—

Getting away from the distractions of the world to spend time alone with God is not as easy as it may seem. We must be intentional about disengaging from the daily chaos. In the silence—that is, the absence of the noise and distractions that make us forget what is really important—we will discover opportunities for recovery, renewal, and clarity.

—o—

Spend an hour or more in total silence. No electronics. No conversation. No distractions. What was difficult about the experience? What was satisfying?

American culture wears busyness as a badge of honor, yet sometimes this busyness is self-manufactured. What busyness can you let go of today?

How has your need for silence changed as you have grown older?

How can you build time for silence into your daily schedule?

In your everyday life, how can you guard against the noise of the world that erodes your well-being?

Clouds

Today I give myself permission to do absolutely nothing.

I have no plans except to rest in the cool ocean breeze.

I am content to watch the sea and sky while listening to the
waves from my front-row seat.

Looking over the top of my sunglasses, I catch an unfiltered view
of clouds floating by in shades of white and pearly gray, like
the graduated hues on a paint-sample card.

Unsuccessfully, I search my memory for the meteorological names
of the cloud formations I learned as a child.

Before long, I study the clouds with maturing eyes that ache to
see truths beyond scientific explanation.

The clouds are the dust of his feet.

The poetic language of scripture reminds me that clouds can
represent God's movement in the world.

I stare at the sky and feel a smile spreading across my face.
Clouds are God's own water-vapor paintings, suspended
in a bright blue gallery, prompting me to look up and
remember those who have gone before me.

Therefore, since we are surrounded by such a great cloud of
witnesses, let us throw off everything that hinders and
the sin that so easily entangles. And let us run with
perseverance the race marked out for us.

A cloud of witnesses: those faithful saints who have gone before
me. Abraham and Moses, my parents and grandparents,
my aunts and uncles. A favorite childhood Sunday school
teacher, longtime church members, neighbors, and friends.

I close my eyes, wanting to focus my mind's eye on each person
who helped mold my spiritual life.

These spiritual ancestors did not abandon their faith when life
was difficult. They felt the sharp pain of rejection and
failure. They suffered illness and grieved the loss of loved
ones.

Still they faithfully embraced the hardships and uncertainties of
life with courage and hope.

Now, as I look up to the clouds, I sense their presence.

Recalling their stories of faithfulness encourages me in the what-
ifs of this season of life.

I can hear them calling to me: "Finish well, dear one."

*Nahum 1:3; Hebrews 12:1 (NIV)

—o—

Scripture is full of references to clouds, most often pointing to the presence of God. Clouds are never still. They move constantly, reminding us of God's faithful movement in the world. Clouds also remind us of the great community of faith that surrounds us, not only people who are physically present in our lives today but also those everyday saints who have gone before us. Wisdom in later life will not come from stagnation or isolation. We need the encouragement and hope provided by our cloud of witnesses for the journey before us.

—o—

Describe a time in your life when you experienced clouds as the dust of God's feet, a reminder of God's work and movement in the world.

Write about a specific time when the strength of another person's faith inspired you to trust God more.

Write the names of ten older saints who already have gone to their eternal rest. Beside each name, list character traits you would most like to emulate as you grow older.

If you could have a conversation with one of these saints, what would you say about your life? What would you want to ask about the journey of aging?

Make a list of younger people upon whom you hope to make a lasting impression such that one day they will look to their own cloud of witnesses and think of you.

Dunes

The only clouds in the sky are a few white and wispy stragglers,
    like errant strands of hair that refuse to obey.

Knotting a towel at my waist, I grab my beach bag and head to
    the walkway that leads me up and over the sand dunes like
    a secret passageway.

With each step, the ocean's waves get louder until, at last, the
    beach is in full view.

A sanctuary of blue and white: sky, sea, sand.

It's a scene that never gets old.

I drop my bag and claim a spot in the sand.

I surrender to the rhythmic sounds of the sea that satisfy a deep
    spiritual need to connect with the Creator.

He is a shield to those whose walk is blameless,

for he guards the course of the just

and protects the way of his faithful ones.

Then you will understand what is right and just

and fair—every good path.

For wisdom will enter your heart,

and knowledge will be pleasant to your soul.

Discretion will protect you,

and understanding will guard you.

In my mind's eye, I retrace my steps over the boardwalk and through the sand dunes, recalling what I read in the guest packet in my room.

Sand dunes are vital to the beach community because they offer the first line of defense against storm surges and high winds.

Just as sand dunes protect their surroundings from storm erosion, God will protect me from the temptations of aging if I steadily pursue God.

Along the journey, I will be tempted to believe that I have outlived my purpose.

There will be days I want to criticize instead of encourage.

There will be moments I want to choose despair instead of hope.

Watch and pray so that you will not fall into temptation. The spirit is willing, but the flesh is weak.

The walk toward wisdom begins with a close relationship with God through prayer and discernment.

Looking out at the expansive sea and sky, I have an acute
    awareness of the Almighty.

Aging is not about gritting my teeth and enduring the hardships.
    It is about living fully with divine purpose, regardless of my
    circumstances.

In the wind and in the waves, I can hear the voice of God calling.

*Proverbs 2:7-11 (NIV); Mark 14:38 (NIV)

— ◯ —

Aging brings with it temptations we may not have considered: a
loss of purpose, an unwillingness to embrace change, a critical
attitude toward younger generations and family members. May the
lesson of the sand dunes encourage us to rely on God's protection
in the difficult moments.

— ◯ —

Write about a situation in which you were tempted to act superior
    toward a younger person because of your age.

With aging may come feelings of isolation, stagnation, stinginess,
    despair, and bitterness. What do you fear most about aging?

Find a Bible verse that focuses on resisting temptation, and write
    it in this journal. Try to memorize it during the next week.

Make a list of five to ten older adults in your life. What are you
    learning from each one about overcoming the temptations
    of aging?

In what ways would deepening your prayer life better prepare you
    to overcome temptations that may come your way along the
    journey of aging?

Footprints

The morning is wrapped in a delicate light and the reassuring
　　sound of the surf.

I take off my shoes so I can feel the sand under my bare feet.

The beach cleanses my soul, allowing me to slough off the worries
　　of life and toss them to the ocean swells.

It is where I attune my heart to God.

As I stroll where the sand and tide meet, I cast my eyes on the
　　footprints ahead.

Imprints in the sand, evidence that others have walked this path
　　before me.

Every now and then, I pause to pick up a shell and drop it into
　　my pocket just as the rush of water covers my feet.

The footprints before me vanish with each surge.

At this thin place where heaven and earth meet, I think about
how fleeting life is and wonder what will remain of me after
my footprints vanish from this world.

The righteous walk in integrity—
happy are the children who follow them.

Looking down at my bright coral toenails, I embrace an
important truth and almost instantly feel the weight of its
responsibility.

I am creating footprints on the hearts and minds of others,
footprints that will last even after my physical body
becomes dust.

I resist the urge to run away from these serious reflections,
and I consider how I am touching the hearts of future
generations.

We will tell the next generation
the praiseworthy deeds of the LORD,
his power, and the wonders he has done.

As I walk back to my cottage, I am mindful of my steps in the
deep sand.

I wonder how I will be remembered after I'm gone from this
earth.

What will my children and grandchildren recall about me in
twenty, thirty, or forty years?

Seeing the footprints dissolve into the sea is sobering yet
somehow makes me feel more vibrant and alive.

It rekindles my determination to share my stories while I still
    can, renews my commitment to living a purposeful life.
Turning back to glance at the sea once more, I notice that the tide
    is getting higher.
I let the sun's rays flood my soul, giving thanks that my legacy
    will leave eternal footprints that never wash away.

*Proverbs 20:7; Psalm 78:4 (NIV)

— ✣ —

So much in life can be washed away in the blink of an eye: cars and careers, homes and health. Even so, those things that last imprint themselves indelibly on the lives of others. We have the opportunity to shape a legacy that will live beyond our span of years. How can we be intentional about creating a legacy of selflessness and faithfulness that will outlive our time on earth?

— ✣ —

Describe how you feel when you see your own footprints in the
    sand wash away.

List five ways you intentionally can shape your legacy.

Pretend that you are eavesdropping on your own funeral.
    Describe the service. What are people saying about you?

How are you using your life to bless to others?

Write a letter to each of your grandchildren, future
    grandchildren, or young family members. Share with them
    a faith story from your life.

night sky

The last light of the day is touching the sea, scattering fragile
golden rays across the water.
The shadows of the evening continue to deepen until the scene
before me finally is enveloped in darkness.
Standing alone on the beach, I let the sound of the pulsing tide fill
my spirit, wishing I could somehow stockpile the serenity of
this moment.
I look up and see the first star of the night winking above the vast
body of water.

Lift up your eyes and look to the heavens:
Who created all these?
He who brings out the starry host one by one
and calls forth each of them by name.

Because of his great power and mighty strength,

> *not one of them is missing.*

The wind breezes through my hair as I place my chair close to
the curling tide and away from the glare of porch lights.

Taking in a deep breath of salt air, my eyes probe the heavens
and my ears listen for the night birds to stir and the cicadas
to begin their serenade.

With the night sky as a backdrop, my mind considers the
transitions that come with aging.

I ponder the unknowns, the twists and turns that await me in the
darkness.

Will I be physically active until my last breath? What if I have to
leave my home? Where will I go? Will I outlive my loved
ones? What if I can't take care of myself? What if I develop
dementia?

The questions pummel me with insecurity.

A quarter moon makes its appearance and hangs over the
darkness of the ocean.

Slowly, the sky is sprinkled with stars that seem close enough to
touch.

I feel a shiver of cool air and reach for a shawl to wrap around my
shoulders.

The LORD is my light and my salvation—

> *whom shall I fear?*

The LORD is the stronghold of my life—

of whom shall I be afraid?

The One who created the stars and the moon will not fail me on
the journey of aging.

The night sky speaks to my heart. It is a constant reminder that
God is near.

I am not alone, even in the darkness.

*Isaiah 40:26 (NIV); Psalm 27:1 (NIV)

— ◉ —

The changes that come with aging can cause worry and fear. So
much of what will happen in the future will be out of our control,
yet we will have a choice about how we respond. May we choose
an attitude of faithfulness, standing strong in the belief of God's
presence in every moment.

— ◉ —

Write about a time in nature when God felt near.

How does nature remind you of God's ever-present faithfulness?

Describe the dominant emotion you feel when you think about
your own mortality.

What brings you peace of mind when you consider the losses and
changes on the journey of aging?

What does it mean to you to "finish well"?

Sandcastles

The sky is cheerfully blue, a perfect backdrop for a sandcastle-
building class on the beach.

I curiously watch as a professional sand sculptor teaches a young
family of five the art of clumping sand and digging moats.

The teacher instructs the parents and children on filling big
buckets with water to make wet, soupy sand, which then is
piled several yards from the tide's reach.

I am intrigued by the technique since I am more accustomed to
kids filling buckets with barely moist sand, patting it, then
dumping it out like a freshly baked cake that quickly cracks.

Watching the activity over the rim of my sunglasses, I notice the
family members working diligently to make a four-foot-high
blob of wet sand that spreads out over a patch of the beach,
looking nothing like a castle.

Then, the instructor brings out an array of makeshift tools and
tells them to start carving the wet sand from the top down.

I burrow down into my chair and start to read my book, trying to
focus on the plot and not the nearby laughter.

When I look up a little later, I see the magnificent fortress they
have created with intricate turrets and moats.

Briefly, I close my eyes and listen to the pure joy in their voices,
even though they know that their sandcastle will soon be
dissolved by the tide.

*This is what I have seen to be good: it is fitting to eat and drink
and find enjoyment in all the toil with which one toils under
the sun the few days of the life God gives us; for this is our
lot.*

The older I get the more I realize that life is all about the journey.

It is about learning to pour energy and love into building
relationships and creating memories without lamenting the
reality that one day this earthly life will be gone.

It is about praising the One who created life in the beginning.

I push up my sunglasses on my nose, giving thanks for the life
lesson before me.

Fully content, I close my eyes and imagine that someone is
looking at the reflection of the finished sandcastle in my
mirrored lenses.

*Ecclesiastes 5:18

—o—

Earthly life is temporary. We all are going to die. Compared to eternity, our lives are just a moment. But joy lived out on earth is a glimpse into heaven. We needn't lose ourselves to despair when we can enjoy our lives today and every day we are on this earth.

—o—

How can you alter your future by thinking of aging as an adventure instead of as a time of decay and loss?

Recount a story of someone you know who is living joyfully in the face of death. What can you learn from his or her experience?

Make a list of ten ways you can add more joy to your life.

Write about a grand adventure you wish to experience before your death. What obstacles are keeping you from making it a reality?

Describe three ways you are demonstrating that you are still teachable even as you grow older.

Souvenirs

The balmy air holds the fragrance of hibiscus, and the clouds
    keep the sun's rays at bay.
I lace up my shoes and walk in the opposite direction of the sand
    and surf, happily heading into the town's center for the day.
Soon the comforting sounds of the ocean give way to the noise of
    local street traffic.
On the corner ahead, I spy a kid-friendly souvenir shop with an
    enormous, opened shark's mouth at the entrance.
I laugh as I recall summer vacations when my children were
    young.
As I draw closer, I feel a nostalgic tug pulling me toward the
    garish tunnel enclosed by shark teeth.
Inside, a flock of life-sized metal flamingos greet me.

I see countless bins of mass-produced knickknacks—magnets,
mugs, and mermaid statues; key chains, inflatable palm
trees, and T-shirts.

Overpriced trinkets that will be quickly broken, forgotten, or
stuck in a closet and ignored.

I pick up a plastic snow globe with a surfing Santa, turn it upside
down, and watch the glitter swirl around.

I can't decide whether to laugh or feel depressed by the
uselessness of it all.

Why do we think we need cheaply made baubles to recall special
moments in life?

Memories of past beach vacations play in my mind like an old
8mm movie reel.

I remember the time I buried silver dollars in the sand and let the
kids excitedly search for them using only their feet.

I reminisce about quiet getaways with my husband to our favorite
secluded beach after our kids had grown.

Only recently had I joined hands with my grandkids to jump
waves together.

Memories like these are a divine gift. I relive each scene in my
imagination and recall the joy.

*I think it is right to refresh your memory as long as I live in the
tent of this body.*

In the busyness of ordinary life, I am quick to forget God's
faithfulness throughout the years.

But these beach memories are rich treasures, reminding me of

family, love, and laughter.

After lunch, I walk back to the beach without a bag full of

knickknacks.

Today I will collect memories, not trinkets. After all, memories

make the best souvenirs.

*2 Peter 1:13 (NIV)

— ◌ —

Remembering special moments from the past can be energizing and inspiring. God grants us the gift of memory so that we can carry our moments with us as keepsakes of time gone by. These rich treasures provide more joy than cheap trinkets. When we remember God's goodness and share stories of God's faithfulness throughout the years, we give a gift of great value to future generations.

— ◌ —

Write about three special memories from your childhood that you

treasure most. How can you share these stories creatively

with younger generations in your family?

Make a list of five specific ways you can be intentional about

collecting memories instead of knickknacks.

Write about something that makes you nostalgic and explain why.

Write about an item that serves as a tangible reminder of God's

love for you.

Describe how what you place value in has changed over time.

Boats and Barnacles

The captain holds out his hand to steady me as I step from
the dock onto the sleek catamaran, helping me keep my
balance aboard the rocking boat.

The exquisite backdrop of sea and sky could easily grace a
postcard.

Soon the boat is gliding effortlessly through the water, and a soft
spray splashes my face as the evening light fades.

I sit back and soak in the scene, watching the waning rays of sun
dance upon the waves.

Just as the sun takes a spectacular final bow and settles into the
deep blue water, the captain gives a long blow on a conch
shell, a tradition that celebrates the end of the day with
gratitude.

*This is the day that the L*ORD *has made;*

 let us rejoice and be glad in it.

Once back at the dock, the captain and mates tie up the boat.

I notice another boat sitting low in the water beside us. Even in

 the dwindling light, I can see that it has been neglected.

Barnacles, the captain explains with disdain. Crustaceans

 permanently encrusted on the surface of the boat, weighing

 it down like concrete blocks.

Without the labor-intensive process of scraping away the

 barnacles, the boat will remain inoperable.

My children, listen to me:

 happy are those who keep my ways.

Hear instruction and be wise,

 and do not neglect it.

In a moment of exceptional clarity, I wonder about what I have

 allowed to build up in my life, what is weighing me down.

I listen to the melodic lap of water against the boats and ponder

 the state of my soul.

As I walk the length of the dock, I turn back to catch one last

 glimpse of the barnacle-infested boat.

I ask myself, What or whom have I neglected?

Am I willing to invite God to strip away my destructive habits

 and negative attitudes?

How can forgiveness and acceptance lighten my spirit's load?

I cannot finish this life well if I am weighed down by the

 barnacles of life.

Even as the questions and darkness surround me, I feel a sense of peace wash over me.

I know that my cleansing will not come at the hands of an angry oppressor but from a compassionate parent whose love knows no bounds.

*Psalm 118:24; Proverbs 8:32-33

— ○ —

As we focus on acclimating to each new life change on the journey of aging, we may forget to attend to our spiritual health. Letting go of emotional baggage and harmful misconceptions that we've accumulated over the years is not an easy task. But we can ask God to help us acknowledge and remove that which weighs us down so we can attend to the spiritual disciplines that will allow us to continue to grow in Christlikeness.

— ○ —

Describe the state of your spiritual health in this season of life.

List five things that have drained life and energy from you this year. Then, list five things that have given you renewed energy and purpose.

Describe a time when you felt close to God. Describe a time when God felt distant.

What changes do you need to make to experience a close relationship with God? What's holding you back?

What spiritual disciplines would you most like to develop — prayer, meditation on scripture, worship, service, fasting, solitude? Why?

Seaweed

This afternoon the ocean has a mixed personality. The churning
water can't make up its mind whether to be vivid blue or
battleship gray.

Clouds are sprinting across the sun, creating a fast-changing
landscape of sunlight mixed with dark shadows.

As I walk the length of the beach, I anchor my hat to my head
with one hand to keep it from blowing away.

Not far from the point where the beach ends and the tall marsh
grasses grow, I notice seaweed washing up on the sugar-
white sand.

I begin to choose my steps more carefully, hoping not to feel the
slimy algae under my bare feet.

It's not long before I decide to turn around and head back to my
  slice of well-groomed paradise where any seaweed has been
  raked and discarded.
Then, I remember something I learned in school decades ago: The
  world needs seaweed.
It is life-giving, oxygen-producing. It is necessary for a diverse
  ecosystem. Without seaweed, many living things would die.
I feel a prick of conscience about my self-centered attitude. Life
  is not all about me. It's not all about my pleasures, my
  preferences, my convenience.

*Do nothing from selfish ambition or conceit, but in humility
  count others more significant than yourselves. Let each
  of you look not only to his own interests, but also to the
  interests of others.*

I look back at seaweed strewn on the sand and consider it a
  warning for the journey of aging.
As I grow older, there will be times when I want to grumble about
  the seemingly unpleasant things of life. There will be times
  when unwanted change interrupts my preferred way of life.
I will be tempted to think that my age somehow gives me license
  to be self-centered and demanding, but it does not.
With the waves lapping my ankles, I stop and open my arms wide.
I throw back my head and breathe deeply, giving little regard to
  anyone who might be watching.

There on the seashore I marvel at how cleverly God uses

something like seaweed to teach me a lesson in humility.

A few moments later when I open my eyes, I notice that the sky is

brighter and the water impossibly blue.

*Philippians 2:3-4 (ESV)

— ❍ —

Sometimes the lens through which we see life may be faulty, incomplete, or simply in need of adjustment. Our perception can distort reality and prompt defensive behavior. May we challenge our perceptions on aging to allow God to bring us fresh insight and understanding.

— ❍ —

Describe a time when you misjudged something or someone.

How have negative stereotypes about aging impacted your experience of growing older?

Describe how your thinking about aging could suddenly change from unpleasant to joyful. What might change your perception?

Write about a time when you performed a selfless act for someone else. How did the experience make you feel?

Describe an older adult you know who is humble in spite of the challenges of aging.

Second Wind

I open my eyes and crawl out of bed, anxious to stroll the beach
while most beachgoers are asleep or are still in their
pajamas, savoring their morning coffee.

By the time I pull on walking shorts and a baggy T-shirt, the
glimmer of first light is waiting outside the door.

Stepping into the soft breeze, the sight of the sea sparkling like
crushed diamonds in the light captivates me.

The sand is cool as I walk barefoot, silently edging past a
charming beachfront inn and a cluster of picturesque
cottages painted in subtle hues, each with an inviting
wraparound porch and a distinctive name.

I feel the warmth of the early sunlight on my shoulders as I
dangle my flip-flops from two fingers.

Walking past the last house on the row, I pause to ponder its
hand-lettered sign: Second Wind.

Even youths grow tired and weary,
and young men stumble and fall;
but those who hope in the LORD
will renew their strength.
They will soar on wings like eagles;
they will run and not grow weary,
they will walk and not be faint.

I come to the beach to catch my second wind, again and again.

In truth, this season of life often leaves me bone-weary.

Ordinary tasks that were once effortless now require more energy
and focus.

Every medical appointment reminds me that my body is changing
and that I am growing older.

I have discovered that it takes no effort to grow old—so long as I
am breathing, I am aging. But aging faithfully is different.

It takes intentional effort and renewed energy to keep my eyes
focused on God while making my way through an ever-
changing world.

When you search for me, you will find me; if you seek me with all
your heart.

I wiggle my toes in the soft sand and tuck the memory of the sign
deep into my heart before turning back.

Each day I am learning to make peace with a body that doesn't look or work like it once did.

Walking back to my own cottage, I realize that I have more vitality in my steps.

In an unexpected gift of grace, I feel the boost of a second wind.

*Isaiah 40:30-31 (NIV); Jeremiah 29:13

— o —

Sports fans often remark that the second half of a game is more exciting than the first. As the clock ticks down, there is a greater sense of urgency and focus. The same might be said about life. We have a God-ordained purpose that never expires. God challenges us to expand our horizons with every passing year. Even as the years come and go, we may find ourselves surprised by a refreshing second wind.

— o —

In what ways can the second half of your life be more interesting and fulfilling than the first?

As you age, you have an opportunity to try new things. What inner whisperings do you hear that encourage you to take on new activities, attitudes, or relationships?

Write about the people into whom you would like to invest your time and energy in this season of life. How will you do so?

Describe your purpose in this current stage of life.

What are you looking forward to in your later years?